Authentic Self-Confidence

Manifest Your Best Life by Embracing Who You Truly Are

Metaphysical Self-Help, Book 2

By Elena G. Rivers

All rights reserved. No part of this publication may be reproduced, stored in a retrieval system, or transmitted, in any form or by any means, electronic, mechanical, photocopying, recording, or otherwise, without the author and the publishers' prior written permission.

The scanning, uploading, and distributing this book via the Internet or any other means without the author's permission are illegal and punishable by law. Please purchase only authorized electronic editions and do not participate in or encourage electronic piracy of copyrighted materials.

Elena G. Rivers © Copyright 2022 - All rights reserved.
ISBN: 978-1-80095-081-8

Legal Notice:
This book is copyright protected—it is for personal use only.

Disclaimer Notice:
Please note that the information contained in this book is for inspirational and entertainment purposes only. Every attempt has been made to provide accurate, up-to-date, and completely reliable information. However, no warranties of any kind are expressed or implied. Readers acknowledge that the author is not engaging in the rendering of legal, financial, health, medical, or professional advice. By reading this book, the reader agrees that under no circumstances are we responsible for any losses, direct or indirect, which are incurred due to the use of the information contained within this book, including, but not limited to, errors, omissions, or inaccuracies. The information provided in this book is for entertainment and inspirational purposes only. If you are struggling with serious problems, including chronic illness, mental or financial instability, or legal issues, please consult with your local registered health care, financial or legal professional. This book is not a substitute for professional or legal advice but simply a collection of spiritual and philosophical concepts to motivate and uplift our readers.

Contents

Introduction – It's Safe to Be You 6

The Power of Authentic Self-Confidence and the Most Common Misconceptions about "Trying to be Confident" 16

Chapter 1 Why Authenticity Is Your Biggest Power (and Its Deep Meaning) 24

Chapter 2 Turning Your "Weaknesses" into Your Strength (Tune into Your Inner Freedom) 46

Chapter 3 The Power of Magnetic Embodiment (Shine Your Light to Attract the Goodness You Deserve!) 56

Chapter 4 The Secret to Unlimited Empowerment (and why you can't fail!) 66

Chapter 5 The Best Way to Save Your Precious Mental, Spiritual and Emotional Energy (and use it to manifest your desires with ease!) 80

Chapter 6 Unleashing Authentically Powerful Worthiness 86

Chapter 7 When Negative Voices in Your Head Can No Longer Control You (and the simple mindset shift to be unstoppable!) 96

Join Our Manifestation Newsletter and Get a Free eBook 104

Introduction – It's Safe to Be You

Hello Beautiful Soul! Thank You so much for taking an interest in this book. My deepest desire is that it helps and empowers you to manifest your best life by embracing who you truly are!

This is what authentic confidence is all about. Rather than trying to be someone you're not to desperately try and get something, while very often, attracting unfavorable circumstances, people, and events, you go through a deeply healing process that helps you unleash your full potential!

No more hiding. No more pretending to be someone you're not. No more seeking validation and approval...

Think of this book as a guide to help you become a powerful thermostat.

Not too sure if this metaphor is very inspiring, but it makes so much sense! As a thermostat, you set your own rules, so your external environment reflects your input.

Unfortunately, the traditional approach to confidence (trying to look confident and pretending someone you're not to gain approval) is more like being a thermometer. You are stuck reacting to your external environment, reflecting its temperature.

This book is not about trying to be persuasive, or influential or making other people do certain things that fit your agenda. Instead, we take a light and authentic approach because by allowing yourself to be you, you will automatically start attracting people, circumstances, and events that resonate with your unique energy.

But before we get any further, let me quickly share my thoughts on the book's cover and title. You see, this book is very close to my heart. While it's not the first (or last) book I've written, it feels so important because I've wanted to write on authenticity and confidence for so long! It felt like I had this book inside me, but I could not find the right words to express it.

So, I gave myself some time and space to heal. While diving into my raw authenticity, I focused on inner work. Everything I discovered I share here, in this book.

This year, the calling to write this book was so strong that I had to stop other projects to sit down and write it.

I know that many things in my life (that, in the past, I considered obstacles or challenges and felt so much resistance towards) happened not to me but *for me* because they helped me build a part of me that can now share this beautiful Authentic Process with others!

I knew I wanted to call my book: *Authentic Confidence* or *Authentically Confident,* and I knew I wanted to focus on deep inner work for lasting change rather than some superficial techniques to help you *look* more confident. There are many other books that take the approach of "how to look confident". Nothing wrong with that; someone may learn how to look more confident and do well in a job interview and change their financial reality. However, from my experience, such an approach is always very short-lived unless a person decides to dive deep, do inner work, and focus on authenticity and long-term transformation.

OK, so like I've mentioned, I wanted to call my book: *Authentic Confidence* or *Authentically Confident.*

Usually, I have a title in my mind before I get down to writing, although sometimes I just sit down and write about what's inside me and then intend to "dress" my words with a suitable title.

But this time, I knew how I wanted to title my book before actually writing it. Something inside me told me to check if there were other books with similar titles, and I realized there were indeed several books about authentic confidence.

Now, I didn't want to publish a book with the exact same title as other authors have written, so I decided to call my book: *Authentic Self-Confidence* to make it a bit different.

I was also pleased to see more people waking up to the power of authenticity and authentic confidence. An interesting thing about my inner transformation (and something I desire to teach you through this book) is that my old self would see other creators or thought leaders as competition. Still, my new self doesn't think in terms of competition anymore. There's no such thing as competition because we can only "compete" with ourselves.

And even that sounds weird! When you get to a place of genuine authenticity, you feel safe, peaceful, and grounded, knowing that you can create whatever you desire in your own unique way. There will always be people who will appreciate your work simply because they resonate with your energy.

That is why you need to stop being afraid of being you. Instead, you must embrace your authentic energy based on your unique skills, talents, and experiences. This book offers a step-by-step process to help you understand and communicate your authenticity to others from a place of calm confidence, coherence, and love.

This works in every situation and every industry!
And it feels so good and peaceful to create from a place of relaxed and pressure-free energy. At the end of the day, we are all messengers of light. We all have different ways of expressing our light. For some, it may be through books and art.

Others may express themselves through inventions. Others may simply choose to shine their authentic light in whatever job they do (and attract extraordinary circumstances thanks to their energy of gratitude and positivity).

Ok, so back to the title. *Authentic Self-Confidence!*
I finally made up my mind and came up with a simple book title.

Even though it's not what I usually do, I decided to test different cover options prior to writing...And when the cover got done, it dawned on me...the word SELF is the biggest and the most important part of this beautiful process! Because it's all about embracing your true self.

1. SELF – understanding who you truly are.

2. Authentic – choosing to embody your true self and show up authentically in all areas of your life.

3. Confidence – the *natural result* of understanding who you are and embodying that with joy, love, and ease!

And that feels good and effortless while helping you attract amazing people, circumstances, and events that are on the same positive vibration!

Hence, the subtitle idea:

Manifest Your Best Life by Embracing Who You Truly Are!

I also got an unexpected idea how to call this new series of books: *Metaphysical Self-Help.*

I love bridging new-age spirituality (energy work and the power of good feelings) and traditional self-development (mindset work, deep focus and action-taking). To me, it's like bridging the feminine and masculine energies, the best of the two worlds! And I absolutely love the audiences and readers such an energetic combo attracts.

But…several years ago, I'd never thought I'd write the way I write. I feared rejection and felt stuck in seeking validation and approval. I kept comparing myself to others and their creative processes while feeling bad about myself, how I was, and how I worked. I always felt like I was missing something or doing something wrong. I kept looking for something outside myself to feel good inside myself. But it would never work. I was stuck in a never-ending loop of not being good enough, waiting (or working extremely hard) for things to change. I was never truly happy.

I think that the way this book is titled will attract people who already understand that true confidence comes from within. But at the same time, I didn't want to turn my work into some kind of a teenage rebellion against what's already out there.

I prefer peace. I'm not here to convince anyone to think exactly like I do, believe in my values, or follow my system. Instead, my intention is to give you tools for self-reflection and inner work to help you awaken who you truly are, realize that it's safe to be you and that there are many people out there who will benefit tremendously from you just being you!

Hence the book's cover background idea- the blue ocean waves. I like it very much. It symbolizes peace and harmony. The steady flow of infinite abundance...The best thing? Even if there's a storm, it never lasts forever...Storms always pass and help us appreciate the joys of peace and sunshine even more!

I feel so excited we're on this journey together and that you attracted this book into your life. I want you to know that working on this book allowed me to reach even more profound levels of inner healing. And since I am writing for you, I feel like expressing my deep gratitude for your presence. Even though technically, we've never met, it feels like we have!

It feels like we've talked about authentic self-confidence over a nice cup of coffee so many times. It really feels like we're on the same journey. And that the ocean we're on is safe and peaceful. It also holds many hidden mysteries of who we truly are so we can keep creating our dream reality with joy and ease.

For now, lesson number one for you is: *it's safe to be YOU*. So, please keep reminding yourself:

I AM safe. I am LOVE. I AM.

And...

It's safe to be me!

Now, I, Elena, am your guide while we embark on this journey together! This book has seven steps and beautiful lessons for you to explore.

Each lesson builds on the previous one. Take your time. There's no reason to rush. First, go through the process and exercises I share in this book at least once. Then, return to this book whenever you feel called to do so, in whatever way you desire (because you will be a different person then, trust me on that one!).

Ready for some authentic transformation? Let's do this!

The Power of Authentic Self-Confidence and the Most Common Misconceptions about "Trying to be Confident".

It's time to own your mind, my friend! Because you decide what and who you let into it. If you find yourself stuck in negative self-talk, questioning yourself, or feeling doubtful, chances are you allowed some toxic energy to jump into your beautiful mind...You got so used to it that it began to feel like something yours!

But here's the good news- negativity was never a part of who you were. Nor were negative opinions of others.

It's time to integrate these fundamental principles:

1. It's not about what other people think. It's about what you think.

Why? It's simple. You create your own reality with your own thoughts, not someone else's. So, always question whatever comes into your mind, and remember that you have the power to reject it. You can trust yourself!

2. Your point of power is NOW, in the present moment.

In fact, realizing and embodying this teaching is the best thing you can do for yourself because you will no longer feel stuck. You can learn from the past and be grateful for it, even for the so-called failures or mistakes. The truth is that you don't fail...Instead, you succeed, or you learn! So, no more living in fear, shame, doubt, or worry.

From now on, I encourage you to take a few mini-mindfulness breaks during the day. Simply allow yourself to slow down for a minute or two. Close your eyes, take a few deep breaths, and tell yourself that your point of power is now in this very moment and that you are a powerful creator (because you are!). Remind yourself that it's safe to be you and embrace your essence.

You can attract everything you truly desire so much faster and with so much more joy and ease if you simply choose to lead with your authentic energy! To lead with your authentic energy, you need to know what you want, who you are, and what you believe in. And your values and beliefs must come from your true, authentic core, not from someone else. Your beliefs need to be positive and empowering and make you feel good while creating harmonious energy around you and inspiring others to be themselves.

True, authentic confidence means no tension, posing, and pretending! So, no more "fake it till" you make it. Remember that we manifest what we hold inside ourselves. So, it's time to make peace with what's inside us so we can shine our true light and keep attracting our desires with joy and ease.

There are so many misconceptions about confidence, such as for example:

-Confidence comes from having something. So, you need to become very successful and accumulate stuff, and then you will feel confident. Well, then, why are there so many famous and rich people who are still insecure?

Genuine, authentic confidence is about believing in yourself independently of external circumstances. So, be OK with what you think you lack. Be good and kind to yourself. Be OK with following your own success process and enjoying it. Validate yourself just the way you are without seeking permission from others.

Here's an example from my life: I am totally OK with pretty slow progress as a blogger. Instead of worrying or comparing myself to others and "how things should be and where I should be by now," I choose to cherish the fact that I do things my way and enjoy creating my own work systems. I create my own standards. Yes, I can definitely learn a lot from successful people in my industry. Still, I am my own guru, and my personal values and authenticity are more important to me than doing things the same way everyone does. I save time and energy because I no longer compare myself to others! Instead, I use my precious energy to show up for my blog readers, keep growing and do my best every day while motivating myself to keep moving forward.

One of the things that conscious manifestors and authentically confident people do is to become aware of their self-talk. Oh, and just a reminder, do so from a place of love. So, whenever you catch yourself with a negative thought, don't punish yourself with more negativity or self-guilt. Simply look at what's going on inside you with self-compassion. Be kind to yourself and quick to forgive yourself for getting off track. Use your self-talk as a powerful tool to soothe your inner states, and keep reminding yourself that you are beautiful, smart, powerful, worthy, deserving and you love yourself.

An authentically confident person is OK with rejection because they no longer seek external validation. So, they don't beat themselves up if they don't succeed at something. Instead, they take a curious look at the lessons learned and how they can improve or do things better. They also fully embody the teaching: "You were not rejected; you were redirected" because they have deep faith in themselves and the creative powers of the Universe. They feel at peace, knowing that things always work out for them in the end, and they don't allow their inner states to be affected by what some people may perceive as failure. Oh, and as I've already mentioned, they own their minds and understand that other people's thoughts and opinions have no power over them. They go inwards and focus on their own thoughts, feelings, and inner states.

When you are authentically confident, achieving success feels fun, and even if there's lots of work to do, you don't feel overwhelmed or burned out. You achieve for yourself and your own satisfaction, not for other people's approval or validation. You love yourself regardless of your achievement, creating an inner state of peace, balance, and health. You also understand that your current trajectory is more important than past results because you allow yourself to focus on your vision and the bigger picture rather than on quick wins just to show off.

As an authentically confident person, you base your self-esteem on your inner state. You are mindful of your choices and actions. Your values and your ability to stick to them make you feel good. You don't depend on achievements or validation from external sources. Sure, you are happy to receive compliments and recognition and are always very grateful for all the support you receive. But, at the same time, you know how to support yourself from within yourself. You have a healthy inner foundation of peace and authentic confidence.

Let's finish this little pre-work chapter with a story that best illustrates the main pillar of authentic vs superficial confidence...

A friend of mine, who is a very successful self-employed professional (and earns 6 figures a year), recently told me:

"I can't imagine how I would feel without my current income. Honestly, I'd probably feel like nobody. I'd feel like I don't exist and don't belong anywhere. I feel so much self-hate now, even though I'm successful. How would I feel if I lost everything? I'd hate myself even more!"

His words made me very sad. And needless to say, I invited him to study the program I'm just about to share with you and, in addition, seek the personalized mental help he needed.

I, too, used to be in a very similar situation. Even though I looked successful and confident on the outside, I felt like nobody on the inside. I lived with a very negative inner "roommate" who constantly questioned my achievements and kept telling me I wasn't good enough. I also lived with a constant fear of losing everything I'd worked so hard for. And so, life felt like a struggle...Things began to change for me when I finally discovered I was living in a self-created prison. And I could choose to leave it whenever I wanted. Just by returning to a beautiful castle of *Authentic Self-Confidence* that was always waiting for me! And now, my intention is to help you re-connect with your own beautiful castle! You're about to return to your fortress and mansion of inner peace and authentic confidence. This formula is the best magnet for manifesting the abundant life you deserve.

Chapter 1 Why Authenticity Is Your Biggest Power (and Its Deep Meaning)

What does it mean to be authentic? Most people would say that to be authentic means to be the real you. This is very, very true! But, there's more to it…

Very few people know that the word "authentic" comes from the Greek word: "authentes" which means to act on its own authority. The word "authentes" is created by two words: "autos" which stands for "self," and "hentes" which stands for being and doing.

I remember how, one night, I suddenly felt a strong impulse to google the phrase "word authentic etymology". And while I do realize that it may seem like nothing special for some people, for me, it felt like a true discovery…

Here's why…

For many years, I felt scared to explore the real, authentic me. For so many years, I was under a deep, limiting belief that I would never be successful in my career and life if I showed up as myself. Instead, I would always look for more and more idols, role models, and online authorities to follow. And while it's always a good idea to keep an open mind, learn from others and allow other people's achievements to inspire us, true success needs to come from the core of who we truly are.

When we create success on our own terms, from a place of authenticity, work feels more fun, and even if we work harder, we don't lose ourselves, our balance, health, integrity, or happiness.

Ever since I discovered the true meaning of the word: "authentic," I turned a part of its definition into an affirmation that I still keep in my wallet, my phone, and on my vision board.

The affirmation is: "I act on my own authority. I am my own authority."

I know that this affirmation is just a positive statement, a collection of empowering words for some people.

And that's fine because everyone has a different story and resonates with different things. But for me, the affirmation that I act on my own authority speaks to every cell of my being and motivates me to keep diving into my authenticity every day. I genuinely hope that it resonates with you and will empower you to *give yourself permission* to be you. Do not let other people's opinions shape who you are. Protect your mind. Yes, sometimes, other people's feedback or beliefs may be helpful and can help you grow. But, if you don't know who you are and are afraid to be yourself, you will just keep drifting in the opinions, wants, and needs of others while losing your authenticity and will to act as your own authority.

So, here's what you can start doing, slowly but surely, starting today! And even if you think you are authentic, there's always the next level. The work of "protecting your own mind" never stops.

Keep asking yourself: "Who am I?". Keep auditing your thoughts, triggers, and reactions, and ask yourself: "Is it mine? Is it really mine? Or am I putting on some kind of a mask to gain approval or to fit in?".

For example, several years ago, I decided to stop complaining. And everything in my life felt so much better! The first step was to stop complaining to others. The second step was to stop complaining to myself. The more I practiced, the better I became at replacing negative thoughts with positive ones. I felt so much lighter and happier. I even experienced more energy just by quitting complaining and using my mental energy to find good in bad and focus on the positive. Now, this tip is nothing new. All self-help, new age, and positive thinking books recommend it. But we all know that putting this stuff into practice requires mental and emotional discipline, especially if everyone around us keeps complaining!

But here's what happened...After several months of sticking to my no-complaining program, I had a family gathering. And on the first day, I complained, just like everyone else around me. Luckily, I was fully aware of what I was doing and stopped. I also realized that I'd indulged in negative behaviors just because I'd wanted to fit in. What triggered my negative behavior was the fear of being judged by a family member who can get pretty toxic and openly laughed at my passion for self-help and self-improvement. Believe it or not, but some people are not into positivity...(topic for another book!)

I share this because I want you to be fully aware of all your behaviors so that you know precisely why you react in a given way. Is it because it's who you indeed are, and it fits into your values and beliefs? Is it congruent with the best version of yourself? Or is it because you're trying to fit in?

Do you change your behavior because you fear other people's opinions or judgments?

Here's what worked for me: *I allowed others to be the way they are.*

My mindset was:

"OK, I told them about my inner work and all the amazing discoveries I had on my self-development and spirituality journey; I wanted to help them. I tried. But I also recognize that I was on a little self-development crusade...."

Whenever I discover something that works for me, whether it's a natural supplement or a healing modality, I feel like telling everyone about it. It's just my nature. I like helping people. And the old me might have been a little bit too intense in assisting people who perhaps didn't want any help or were not ready to change. On the other hand, sometimes, I would reverse back to my old negative behaviors to experience unity and closeness with some old friends or family members. So, I was lowering my own standards. And when you drop your standards, you're not helping anyone...

After realizing this, I looked deeper into my values and how I wanted to do things and position myself to the Universe.

I strongly recommend you adapt my strategy to your own values; I just share what works for me.

If I see that someone might benefit from my knowledge or wisdom, I make a recommendation (it can be a book, a system, a program, or a simple tip or technique). If I see they get interested, I carry on. But if they get resistant or critical, I know they are not ready. So, I tell them: "OK, I understand. If you ever change your mind, let me know."

It makes me feel good that at least I did my part and tried to help. But, at the same time, I don't bother others with unsolicited feedback or advice.

My other rule is to keep my inner work to myself. I only share what I do in my books or with people who are into spirituality, manifesting, and self-development.

I intend to treat all my family and friends with love and respect. I do my best to spread uplifting energies and support everyone the best I can. This is why I don't join anyone in complaining. I simply try to talk about something positive. From my experience, what works best is to have a nice collection of happy or funny memories and direct the topics of conversations to those. It makes everyone happy and strengthens the family bond. It just feels so good for everyone!

And it doesn't make me lower my standards and indulge in complaining. At the same time, it doesn't make me show up as some superior self-development crusader. The conversations naturally focus on happy events and gratitude, so there's no space for arguments. Keep it peaceful, keep it natural, and stick to your standards!

This is a simple example of how we can stick to our values and be authentic while creating a peaceful environment without pretending to be someone we're not just to fit in.

So, release who you think you *should* be to gain approval. In most cases, trying to be someone you're not will only lead to unwanted events and circumstances. It may also make you feel bad. I don't know about you, but whenever I would reverse back to my old, negative patterns, I felt bad for not honoring my values. Luckily, I finally learned my lesson, so all is good!

You really need to believe in yourself and the power of your own authenticity. You become magnetic when you choose to shine your true light wherever you are. When you show up as your true, authentic self in any situation and act on your behalf as your own authority, the Universe will take notice! Sooner or later, people will realize you have your own values and will feel inspired by you. Your authentic embodiment will empower them to shine their true light as well. Because it's safe, magical, and fun. It really feels good.

As an extra bonus, it's such an inner energy saver. Before my personal transformation, I often felt mentally tired and energetically drained (even though my diet and physical health were perfect).

It's because most of my thoughts were centered around what other people thought of me, how I was perceived and how I should behave. My thinking was: "How would they want me to behave? What would they want me to do or say? Let's put another mask on. Oh, wait, what if they don't like it? What if I don't do it right?"

It was so exhausting. I begin to feel tired just writing about it! Now, this process is not always easy, and as my story illustrates, sometimes you may be tempted to reverse back to your old ways of being just to fit in. Here's my tip, when that happens, don't feel bad. Forgive yourself and move on.
Simply acknowledge that you are now fully authentic, and be compassionate about yourself and others.

There is always something to learn about yourself! So, approach all your fallbacks from a place of curiosity and self-love. Be grateful because triggers are healers, and we always get presented with people, situations, and circumstances to show up as our true selves. It's all about practice! Another thing I highly recommend you begin reflecting on is your relationship with success and achievement. Why do you desire success? Is it because you want to impress others? Authentic success is much better because it is a natural extension of the harmonious expression of your energy, talents, and skills. Remember that any industry can be revolutionized, so if you desire to do something new in your field, go ahead and do it. Don't deny your unique ideas. Don't hide behind excuses such as:

"But, in my industry, this is unheard of..", or: "But nobody is doing it...". Instead, give yourself permission to be a revolutionary in everything you do while respecting yourself and others.

Let's dive deeper into the main difference between authentic and inauthentic confidence.

What about: "Dress for success"? This phrase is often thrown around in success, business, and self-development cycles. And yes, some industries may require a particular dress code.

But losing your authenticity or blindly following through is never a must. Allow yourself to pursue your own taste. In other words: *Dress for yourself. Dress to feel good!*

For example, going for specific designer clothes just to fit in, or just because your friends or colleagues wear them is not authentic. However, if you like a specific brand and feel good about it, the decision comes from your taste for fashion and personal standards.

Inauthentic confidence can be compared to living a surface life, and it accurately describes how I used to live.

On the outside, my life seemed terrific, and everyone congratulated me on my success and achievements. But deep inside, I felt insecure and constantly feared losing everything. I always needed a distraction, such as a party, travel, or a shopping spree, because I felt empty inside. The negative chatter inside me was filled with constant: "What if they don't like it…", "What if they don't approve."

I didn't have any boundaries either. So, I'd just fit in…. And my surface-level confidence lifestyle kept attracting surface-level people.

But when my mental health began to suffer, I knew I had to change something. And the change had to come from the inside. I knew I had to do what I'd been so afraid of for years. I had to give myself permission to be me. I had to be OK with being imperfect. I had to develop self-empathy and attract like-minded people into my life. My old self used to see authenticity as a weakness, something I had to work hard to hide. But my new self saw it as a sign of courage and something to be proud of. It all starts with self-acceptance. Daily self-acceptance! So, keep auditing your everyday choices, thoughts, and motivations. Put your authenticity first.

Remember that weakness is not the end of the world. Nor is failing or making mistakes. Just do the best you can with what you know and keep growing.

Following this simple, authentic self-confidence formula helped me transform all areas of my life. It made me realize that I could trust myself and make the right decisions. And I no longer waste my time trying to become successful according to other people's standards of success. I can always learn a thing or two from a new online mentor, but I am free to make my own decisions based on my personal preferences. I want the same for you, and I truly hope my story alone can awaken you to your authentic power. Because it can help you become unstoppable!

Here's another example from my life: Several years ago, I made a simple decision to focus on what I loved – my writing. I knew I had a message to share. I knew I wanted to inspire people by providing them with manifestation and spirituality concepts that changed my life. But at first, I got very distracted by what everyone else was doing.

Some people were doing speaking events and retreats. Some were doing online courses. Some were on YouTube or Facebook ads. And I mistakenly thought I had to do precisely the same strategy they were doing because then I'd be successful (or better said: perceived as successful). So, in the end, I got distracted by the shiny object syndrome and self-sabotaged my writing efforts. Luckily, I woke up and decided to stick to what I had always wanted to do. I understood that everyone is different and everyone has a different preference when it comes to self-expression. I also fully embraced the fact that I am a nerdy introvert and love it. At the same time, I met many people who were great at speaking and loved organizing live events. But for some reason, they forced themselves to hide and write, even though they didn't like it, just because they thought it was somehow required.

You know, the mindset of: "First, I need this so that I get approved for that, and then I will finally be able to...." Now, such a mindset may be necessary in some situations, professions, or career/ business choices. But, from my experience, we can allow ourselves to do what we love and feel like it's a part of our DNA.

Stick to your own thing, and do what makes your heart happy. Focus on what you're naturally good at and make it your main thing. You can still try and test other things or challenge yourself to overcome your weaknesses. But first of all, focus on developing your natural talents and what aligns well with your personality. Be patient. Allow yourself the space to fail. Doing what you love is not always easy and requires passion and perseverance. But...it also gives you a tremendous amount of peace. That feeling is with you 24/7, the feeling of choosing yourself and doing the right thing. The feeling of following through with your own choices and standards, the sense of creating your own path.

The only person that stays with you 24/7 is you...So you'd better feel good about yourself! Why worry so much about what other people think? It's all about what *you* think. Nothing beats the feeling of authentic happiness based on allowing yourself to live according to your life philosophy.

The Raw You wears no mask. *The Raw You* is built on self-trust and self-compassion. *The Raw You* is not afraid to admit what they know or don't know. There is no need to embellish your achievements or try to do something to be perceived in a certain way...

Authenticity is so refreshing, and it always wins. People love authentic people. Most people want to be themselves and would love to create a life and career as a natural extension of who they are. So, when they see someone already living an authentically confident life they may get inspired. They ask themselves what it would be like to stop hiding or being ashamed of their shortcomings?

An online world can be a great example of inauthentic behaviors just to fit in. And, as I've already told you, I've also fallen into that trap...I tried to be someone I wasn't to achieve success defined by some online guru standards, and trust me when I say this – it was a constant roller coaster, and I could never create lasting success or fulfillment.

Because we can't succeed as someone's clones. It's our unique energy and set of skills that make us special. A good question for self-reflection is: *Why* do you want to do something?

Is this desire coming from your heart, curiosity to test something new, or is it because everyone else is doing it? Start practicing making your own choices based on your true, authentic desires.

I used to be like a chameleon, desperately trying to fit in. I was a thermometer. Not a thermostat. And it was so exhausting! Then, I felt ashamed because I wasn't being me. But that shame had value because it eventually opened my eyes to the power of authenticity and how good it felt.

Inauthentic confidence only led to misalignment.

Here's the obstacle I experienced on my journey…

I already knew I wanted to re-create myself or, better said, get back to who I really was (without having to put another mask on!). And, to do so, I had to release the feeling of "not-enoughness" because the old me mistakenly believed that it wasn't safe to be authentic and that nobody would love me…

In a way, my old self was creating a self-fulfilling prophecy. I didn't love and accept myself and could not attract unconditional love and acceptance…When I say "unconditional love and acceptance", I'm not referring to romantic love alone, but also love coming from people you work with, your friends, or community.

You can release fear by accepting it and changing your relationship with it. It's safe to be you. Nobody can judge you, and you have the right to be yourself. It is your birthright. And by choosing to be yourself, your life can only change for the better.

Also, remember that it's safe if not everyone likes you.
People are free to make their own choices and create their own tribes. Why would you want to attract people who don't resonate with your values? Holding space for your new authentic self and people who respect it is much better. Putting on a mask is like wasting your natural energy and instead trying to attract something that is not even good for you. Choosing to be yourself and loving yourself the way you are open the gate to inner peace. There's no more resistance.

Besides, you can inspire others through your authentic achievement and your energy. You don't have to be perfect. Just be yourself and do what you know how to do with your best energy. Keep improving and moving forward but remember that you act on behalf of your own authority.

I can't even tell you how many times I bought something from teachers and coaches whose websites or social media profiles were not perfect, and they were not the best speakers or writers. The information they shared was not new to me, but I loved how they communicated and taught it. I loved their energy, uniqueness, and how they showed up. I loved their calm and their authentic confidence, and how they ran their businesses.

They felt safe to be them! And so, others felt safe around them, contributing to the atmosphere of peace. It's safe to be you. Stop judging and criticizing yourself. Also, remember that individuals who choose to judge and criticize you reflect their own insecurity. Know that you're safe! When others judge you, in most cases, it's about them. That should give you some courage while facing your fears.

From my experience, toxic people will fade away when you're focused on YOU and don't give them your power or energy. After all, that's why they are after your precious energy! They need their energy supply because they're empty inside. The best way to cut them off is to focus on your personal growth while living according to your own life philosophy.

Also, allow yourself to celebrate your success. Don't worry. It's not the same as bragging. Authentic confidence is not about bragging or making others feel bad. By choosing to celebrate your achievements, you inspire others and make them feel good, so they can do their best in life. From my perspective, the best way to celebrate authentically is to share the lessons you learned on your path to success. This is how others can get value from your achievements and learn from you. It doesn't feel like you're trying to be superior and boast about how awesome you are while making others feel inadequate. So, combine each success celebration you make (whether it's having a party or an online gathering) with a little presentation of everything you've learned on your journey. Act like a love-based, kind-hearted leader that inspires others. All you need to do is to be authentic and share.

Inauthentic, forced confidence is toxic and stems from deep insecurity. A person who feels insecure may feel the need to brag about their success in an attempt to make others feel less significant. Authentic confidence, however, is about fully embodying who you are and creating success as a natural extension of your uniqueness. Others can see that you're a person who's resilient, self-motivated, passionate, and never gives up. They also realize you're a human who also encounters setbacks and obstacles. All you need to do is to show up as you and do the best you can with what you know.

Never lower your vibration to fit in or gain approval. Release the need to gossip to be accepted, and have your standards for all areas of your life. For example, after setting up my health standards and self-care boundaries, I no longer felt the need to go out, drink and indulge in gossip and drama. Yes, every now and then, I enjoy going out for nice dinners with true friends, people who respect me for who I am. I enjoy a nice glass (or two) of wine with my meal. But I no longer go out the way I used to. You know, following other people's standards, then paying it off with a hangover and feeling bad about myself.

Back then, I wasn't even fully aware that I could consciously choose the people I wanted to attract into my life. Instead, I was too busy trying to fit in...Then, I would often complain about the people disrespecting me or gossiping about me behind my back. It was a negative, self-inflicted cycle stemming from the fact that I lacked boundaries, didn't know who I was and what I truly wanted, and didn't give myself permission to be me.

One important lesson I learned is that wishing for others to change is pointless because your energy is better spent on inner work and authenticity. For example, we may make detailed lists of what kinds of people we wish to attract into our lives and how we wish to be treated. However, if we don't work on ourselves and don't create and respect our own boundaries and life philosophy, chances are we will keep attracting the same old patterns.

So, give yourself some time and space to be you. Envision all areas of your life and how you choose to show up and treat yourself and others. Give yourself some time to do this exercise. You may even decide to do it several times or come back to it after you finish this book. Release any fears based on your past conditioning or the need to get approved, look good, or be validated.

Let this quote guide you and embody your true self in a naturally confident way:

"As we are liberated from our own fear, our presence automatically liberates others" – Marianne Williamson

The Authentically Confident You Exercise (Your Life Philosophy):

1. What makes you truly happy? What brings joy into your heart?
2. How do you want to be remembered? What do you wish to be known for?
3. What do you really value in life?

4. What does your ideal workday look like?
5. What does your perfect holiday or day off look like?
6. What are your past mistakes? What did you learn from them? Did they make you a better person?
7. What traits do you value in others? Do you embody these traits yourself?
8. How do you take care of your physical body? Do you have firm self-care standards and boundaries?
9. How do you take care of your mindset and emotions? What kind of inner work do you enjoy?
10. How do you take care of your spiritual life? Do you embody your spiritual views?
11. What are you naturally good at? Do you give yourself the time to develop your talents?
12. What do you value in your professional life and the people you work with? Do you embody these traits and qualities too?

If you feel a bit stuck, don't worry. Authentically re-creating yourself while removing old layers that no longer serve you may take some time. Don't rush through this process. Enjoy it!

In the next chapter, you will discover a simple but effective tool for unlimited peace and inner freedom!

Chapter 2 Turning Your "Weaknesses" into Your Strength (Tune into Your Inner Freedom)

Have you ever got stuck in a cycle of buying different courses or programs and not getting results? I know I have! And, what's interesting, in most cases, I could not blame the course creators…My problem with getting results was due to the fact I could not really follow instructions. I know it sounds bizarre! I would invest in a program mainly because I wanted a step-by-step strategy.

But when I was already in a program, I found it very hard to follow its instructions. The reason? I was too much in my head. For example, I would start thinking about the courses I'd bought in the past while experiencing extreme levels of self-guilt for not getting results or not following through.

Sometimes, I would follow through a bit, get some results and then quit and use an excuse of: "It wouldn't be worth it long-term anyway because this strategy will stop working very soon."

At the same time, it was hard for me to socialize and create deep connections because I found it hard to listen to others. I was immersed in my negative mind chatter, so busy thinking about what to say or what others thought of me! Instead of just chilling out and mindfully following the conversation while enjoying the gift of being a listener and getting to know someone, I would get stuck in my head, desperately thinking about the right thing to do or say...

That was before my personal transformation. Because now I understand and cherish the gift of being present...And it's so simple. You just need to remember to do it. Just remind yourself that it's OK to be fully present and it's OK to listen. Also, let me share a little secret: most people are too busy thinking about what others think of them. And most people love talking about themselves. So, even if it's hard for you to be at the center of the conversation, you can always allow yourself to listen to other people, ask questions and be fully present.

I'd also recommend you start to integrate these two powerful teachings:

1. Stop worrying about what to say, what others will think of you, and how you will be perceived. Instead, focus on the present moment and listen to what others say.

2. Allow others to be themselves, and release any judgment or criticism. Integrate a neutral state of being. Remember that nobody can hurt or judge you, and you have the right to be yourself. Yes, there might be some toxic people who, for some reason, enjoy throwing others off balance. But, as they say: "What others do is their karma. How you react to it is yours" (not too sure who the author of this quote is, but I heard it many times, and it resonated with me). The main point is - nobody can get to you without your permission!

In other words, be yourself and allow others to be themselves. Welcome and accept them the way they are. Use the gift of the present moment, and focus on listening to others. You will soon notice how your relationships improve before your very eyes!

You will also liberate yourself from unnecessary mental activity and fears of saying or doing the wrong thing. Of course, when I share this teaching, I assume you are a kind, empathic and compassionate person and will not use authenticity as an excuse to "speak your mind" so that it hurts others. Believe it or not, I met some people who think they are authentic by going on self-centered rants to bash and ridicule others. Needless to say, that's not what we want to do.

Releasing the need to worry about saying the right thing feels so good and liberating. No more feeling stressed out about social occasions! All there is to "worry about" is embracing the present moment and our true essence. We are infinite beings having a temporary experience on Earth while exploring our full potential and authenticity.

If you ever find yourself too much in your head, focus your attention on your heart. Take a few deep breaths and enter your heart. Remind yourself that in your heart, you're safe!

Now, this chapter was supposed to be the end chapter of this book. But for some reason, I felt inspired to share it as the second step in this process because I believe it will make your journey so much easier and fun. Many people (my old self included) might feel stuck with inner work because, once again, they are too much in their head, whether they are doing it right or what they did or shouldn't have done in the past. All these are unnecessary guilt-trips that only take your power away.

And let me get you in on a little secret...because if you're reading my book (or books), I assume you're into manifesting, metaphysics and law of attraction.

Well, one of the best things you can do on your manifesting journey is to be less in your head and more in your heart while cultivating feelings of inner peace. Try it yourself. Most people who have tried this technique (if we can even call it a technique) report that the mere suggestion of being more in their hearts fills their whole bodies with calmness. It feels like their problems and worry begin to dissolve (and many so-called "issues" are no longer perceived as issues).

If you're too focused on yourself and how to make an excellent first impression, you risk putting on a mask again. First, accept yourself the way you are. For example, I am pretty shy by nature, and I am an introvert. I used to try to hide it. On many occasions, I would drink too much to seem more confident and chatty. Bad idea!

But once I embraced and accepted my shy, introverted nature and began showing up as myself while embracing the present moment, I discovered I could be a great listener. By being a great listener, I learn about and understand human nature and make authentic connections with people.

My old "friends," or better said, people, I unconsciously attracted into my life (because I wasn't being myself), would often laugh at my introverted nature. They made rude remarks and tried to change me. However, my new friends (and the people I consciously attracted into my life by embracing *the Real Me*) love and respect me the way I am. They appreciate my lifestyle and what I do and don't try to change me into an outgoing person. They understand I am a great companion for a small gathering/ picnic/ yoga class/ meditation retreat, or hiking. I also get fantastic ideas for books and articles just by tuning in and listening to others. I only wish I'd dared to be me sooner (like twenty or even thirty years ago, haha!)

But at least I got to experience different extremes, and I now know what's good for me. I encourage you to take the same approach. Don't beat yourself up for your past inauthentic behaviors. Back then, you didn't know what you know now. And your behaviors were most likely "autopilot behaviors".

We all desire to be loved, respected, and a part of a supportive community. Nobody wants to end up alone. And everyone always does their best with what they know. When we are not fully aware of who we are, our behaviors might get inauthentic and driven by the need to fit in. But there's always a way out.

When you get on the other side of fear -the fear of being you - your old life, and your old self will get a new meaning. You will be able to turn your old, unfavorable circumstances into your life philosophy or even teachings that can help others on their journeys.

When you are authentically confident, your self-worth comes from inside you, and you feel rooted and grounded in who you are. It's not the same as being flashy or arrogant trying to prove one's worth to others (while belittling others), as a toxic person might do in an attempt to look confident.

When you're authentically confident, you embrace self-love as a way to express yourself freely, even if you think you're not perfect. You are honest about what you can or cannot do. At the same time, an inauthentic person might use self-love as an excuse for indulging in complacency or self-absorption. Some may even think "self-acceptance" is about being purposefully lazy or not putting in enough effort.

An authentically confident person is not afraid to admit their mistakes. They know that the mere realization of not doing the best they could or making a mistake is a lesson in itself, and they can use it to learn, grow, improve, and do better next time.

Finally, an authentically confident person is not bothered by the past or future. They cherish *the here and now* and value it as their most significant gift and point of power.

Mindfulness means self-respect, and when you respect yourself, you automatically know how to respect others. You are in the present moment. You respect yourself, others, and the precious gift of life. What you focus on expands.

If all you focus on now is cherishing the present moment and doing whatever you do with love, your life will change.

The present moment helps us shift from:
-self-guilt;
-shame and embarrassment;
-inability to move on;
-being stuck in unhappiness, anger, and frustration

The skill of mindfulness will help you transform your "weakness" into power. It's one of the most incredible skills you can master and so helpful for those on a metaphysical journey of the law of attraction, manifestation, and authentic self-confidence!

You are in charge, and you can always choose to shift and embrace a more positive and empowering state! First of all, be grateful for your power to choose.

Then, ask yourself:
-"How long do I want to stay in this negative energy?"
-"Can I choose to do something more empowering and be in the present moment?"
-"Is my life worth wasting on those disempowering states?"

Yes, they want to show you something...And you may want to use them in an empowering and mindful way so that they serve you! Keep reminding yourself that you can always choose. Triggers are healers and not the end of the world. Surely but steadily, you're walking into the best version of yourself because this is how it's supposed to be. Being fully present and grateful go hand in hand. Both can be used to facilitate a fantastic transformation and help you shift. Even what seems like an unfavorable situation may be used as a channel for change.

For example, you didn't get the job or promotion you wanted. But what if it was meant to happen because something better awaits you? You can choose to embody this mindset and really feel it in all cells of your body, *right here and now*.

The more you love and accept who you are and own who you are and your worth, the easier it is not to let anything outside you affect your state, and what you desire to manifest.

Chapter 3 The Power of Magnetic Embodiment (Shine Your Light to Attract the Goodness You Deserve!)

Authentic self-confidence is about unconditional love and acceptance toward yourself and others. Easy said than done, I know! If you've been around spirituality and self-development for longer than five minutes, you already know the importance of releasing judgment.

But until we fully embody what we discover, we keep getting triggered and walking away from what we learn. Now, spirituality and self-development are a journey that requires investment. There's an investment of time we spend to absorb all the information from books and programs. And then, there's also the money we spend on books, courses, mentors, and seminars.

So, why not treat our investment with the respect it deserves? This little mindset shift was a big *aha* moment on my journey because it inspired me to embrace the next step of transformation. I had to embody the concepts that resonated with me.

Instead of talking to everyone about the self-development techniques and concepts I was learning about and then showing a massive discrepancy between what I intellectually knew and embodied, I had to step into the *New Me*! I'm sure you can relate...We have all been there.

This chapter is about loving and accepting yourself unconditionally so you can fully embrace the next step - the magnetic embodiment! My deepest intention behind writing this chapter is to give you a sense of inner liberation and help you release the layers of shame, guilt, "not-enoughness," and all the self-imposed shackles of our minds.

It's time to leave all that behind! Oh, and the mindset and energy shifts you will experience in this chapter will help you make the most out of any investment you make in yourself, whether it's a book, course, coaching, or whatever you choose.

So...what stops us from embodying what we learn? There are a few reasons, such as:

-Perfectionism to fit into someone else's standards;
-Thinking that someone had it easier than you;
-Worrying about what others will think when you choose to embody what you learn.

For example, you may study LOA and understand the importance of releasing the need to complain. But then, you hang around with friends who complain and feel tempted to succumb to that familiar yet disempowering feeling.

Judgments are subjective, and everyone can have their opinion. Better to be happy and cohesive with your embodiment than to lose your energy trying to be right, convince others or make them feel and think the way you do.

Stop trying to be perfect. Instead, embrace progress. We've already covered the importance of the present moment.
Right now, you are free from judgments and can be you.

The next moment, you will mindfully choose to do the same. Tomorrow. Day after tomorrow. And for eternity, because this is who you are!

After releasing the need for perfection, one of the shifts I experienced was becoming a pretty prolific writer and creator. Because now, when I write, I focus on the joy of sharing, and I think about my readers and how to uplift and help them shift their consciousness (without trying to convince them to feel exactly like I do or persuade them into something).

Words like "persuade" or "convince" are no longer in my vocabulary. Instead, I embody who I am, and I share about it. I may not be perfect about how I do it, but that's OK. It's OK to be raw as long as you are coherent with your authentic being. Make friends with your imperfections and welcome them. Allow yourself and others to be exactly as they are!

Embrace both the positive and the negative. Our negative side is just feedback from our Higher Self and the Universe...

Be vulnerable! Accepting your imperfections allows you to create authentic and meaningful connections with others. People love connecting with other people. And this rule applies to any industry. So many people chase success and want to improve their careers by following industry standards. As if it was some set law! Well, why not create your own rules and standards?

Once again, as long as your rules are ethical and don't harm anyone, you're good to go. Don't allow the negative opinions of others to stop you. Let them wash over you. Yes, other people can express their beliefs. That's fine. But, you stick to your vision based on your desires.

Also, if someone constantly expresses negative opinions towards you, it's most likely about themselves. It may be time to start protecting your time and space from negative individuals. Simply let them go and focus on people who respect you. You begin with self-respect, self-love, and self-acceptance!

One thing I want you to start practicing is to stop explaining and justifying yourself. You will save time and energy, and at the same time, you will free yourself from many harmful and toxic people. Your energy and time are best spent on being you or learning who you truly are. And it's hard to do so if you're constantly pressured into being someone you are not to make people (who might not even care about you) happy.

Because people who genuinely care about you will be happy to see you transform and shine! Take pride in who you are physically, emotionally, spiritually, and mentally. Below are some examples...

Clothes and make-up are tools to accentuate who you are, your style, and your personality. Their aim is to make you feel comfortable. As we've already concluded in the previous chapters, you can dress for success, yes, but remember to define your success! The old me, however, would use make-up or clothes almost as a disguise or costume. I didn't even allow myself to entertain the thought of what I really wanted to wear and what made me feel good.

Also, be you spiritually. Embody your beliefs and live by them. Don't be ashamed of them. Don't hide anything. And don't use fake positivity or spirituality to mask what you perceive as imperfections, either. One of the biggest misconceptions in the self-development/ LOA circles is that you must always be positive, and every negative moment is a deadly sin.

Now, I know I'm exaggerating a bit...But I am sure you can relate. I've said it so many times in my other books. Yes, of course, we want to be positive. Authentically Positive! The word authentic also stands for self-acceptance, so even if you experience something negative, allow yourself to feel through the negative emotions. Don't mask them from the fear of being labeled as negative. We are all human, and we are here to experience contrast.

Likewise, take full ownership of every time you mess up or get triggered. Embrace your triggers. That's OK. Triggers are healers. Now you have a map that tells you where not to go, and you also have something to work through (hey, that's what self-development is all about!).

Finally, forgive yourself for all the "bad money decisions" We have all made them. Instead of beating yourself up, take a piece of paper and write down everything you have learned about money thanks to your past mistakes. Then, release all the past drama. Instead, focus on the inner strength and wisdom that your past "bad money decisions" actually gave you. Now you can make good decisions, and you can trust yourself.

Repeat the same process with other areas of your life, such as your: career, relationships, health, and fitness. Turn self-guilt and self-pity into full acceptance and wisdom through gratitude. An authentically confident person knows the art of embracing challenges as an opportunity to grow. This brings us to the next level of embodiment! Even though I am sure most of my readers know and do this already, some people may benefit from a little reminder.

Stop using words such as: "trouble," "problems," "horrible," and "terrible." These words make us indulge in a victim mindset and imply that things happen to us and that we are powerless. Instead, just say "a challenge" or "an opportunity to learn and grow." I also like the expression: "A chance to grow my emotional muscles."

One of my favorite affirmations for this process is an affirmation I learned from Louise Hay: "All is good in my world!". It fills my heart and mind with feelings of safety and peace.

Another affirmation I love is by Vadim Zeland: "Everything is unfolding exactly as it should!". Because it makes us believe that things always work out for us in the end. Challenges are a part of our human experience here on Earth. But we can also use them to tap into the hidden strength we didn't even know we had inside us.

That little shift alone will help you embody the energy of growth, expansion, and progress. It will also help you embody the power of inner work and transformation; after all, one of the most life-changing metaphysical secrets is that of inner work. As you change yourself, your world changes.

Go through challenges without shame or judgment.
When you embody the above truths, you will automatically radiate empathy and compassion toward others. When you stop judging and shaming yourself, you don't feel like judging or shaming others. Instead, you feel incredible oneness, harmony, connection, and love!

Hurt people hurt people. It may be tempting to get back at someone. It may be tempting to get triggered, but that only puts us behind and negates all our positive inner work.

Remember what we said about our investments. Imagine you invest in stocks or property. Naturally, you would want returns on your investment and never choose any actions you knew would make you lose your money. The question is:

Why do we decide to deflate the investments we make in ourselves?

I believe that the best investment we can ever make is in ourselves. It's time to take this seriously; it all starts with self-acceptance and making peace with ourselves so we can honor and fully embody our values.

Chapter 4 The Secret to Unlimited Empowerment (and why you can't fail!)

The wisdom contained in this chapter will help you shift your mindset and energy in such a way that any remaining vibrations of victimhood will be transformed into victory.

Of course, this is not a onetime event but a life-time process. So, I invite you to read through this chapter more than once. At the same time, keep scanning your awareness for any victimhood energies with a firm intention of releasing them.

Because when you get rid of victimhood vibes, you no longer attract victim circumstances. Now, this may sound very harsh to some people, and it definitely did sound harsh to me when I first discovered it. But no matter what life throws at us, I believe we can always move forward and change at least one thing in our lives that will help us climb the ladder of positivity and higher vibration.

Remember that your main job is to reflect what you desire to attract. So why would you consciously choose to reflect victim or drama queen vibes?

Before we get into this work, here's my little disclaimer: it is not my intention to belittle anyone's trauma or what they have been through in their lives. And I'm not implying that they consciously manifested whatever negative things happened to them and it was all their fault. Not at all. And I don't want to gaslight or victim-shame anyone into "fake positivity". My goal is to empower people so that they can focus on the positive transformation they deserve. I will also add that some people may benefit from talking to a professional therapist or counselor to heal some of their past traumas. I'm not saying you should reject any conventional mental health treatments.

The work I teach in this book is spiritual, energetic, and mindset work to help you be in charge of your life *now* and create a better life in the future by allowing you to focus on your vision and the best version of yourself. Its main focus is on what you can create *in spite of* whatever unfavorable circumstances you experienced. As one of my mentors put it beautifully: "Successful people achieve success not *because of* favorable circumstances but because of the inner resilience they cultivate *in spite of* the negativity they encounter." So, my main message is that even if you experienced unfavorable circumstances in the past, or got hurt, you can *still* be successful and manifest your desires!

Now, with that little mindful disclaimer out of our way...Let's take a few deep breaths and take an honest but loving look at ourselves. No judgment. No blaming. In fact, we're entering a reality where there's no such thing as blame! You can't blame yourself, and you can't blame others. All you can work with is *the power of now* and authentic transformation.

Because a truly authentically confident person doesn't blame people, things, or outside circumstances...

You are not doomed to an inevitable fate or circumstance because of some mysterious force or bad luck. Nothing is wrong with you. You just cling to old, outdated beliefs that no longer serve you. You always have a choice. You can choose full ownership or full victimhood. But ownership is where you can find power and healing.

Adverse circumstances and challenges can be feedback to realign and recharge your faith. But when you blame other people or circumstances, you are giving your power away. You are hopeless. And by the Law of Attraction, you send the message to the Universe:

"Look at me; I am so powerless and such a victim. I love blaming and complaining. Not that I openly say I do, but this is what I do through my actions, thinking, and energy. All the time. It's my predominant vibration; deep inside, I love it because it feels familiar. Please send me more victim vibes and something to complain about! Being in this energy makes me relatable to my friends. Now we are in this victim vibe together and can devote entire gatherings and re-unions to complaining!"

Does that sound familiar? I know I am exaggerating here, but it's just to accentuate my point...

Ownership is when you admit that something went wrong, learn from it, accept all the feelings generated through it, and move on as a wiser person. That's it. Really simple!

Be honest about any time you messed up. And turn these mess-ups into lessons. We're all human, and we all make mistakes. As you learn from a mistake, it's no longer a mistake; it becomes a lesson and it empowers you. You choose how to respond to anything...

Pain can become purpose, pleasure, and passion.

Use your God-given ability to transform negative into positive, and you'll never be a victim of circumstances. You can always choose to unleash your strength or weakness. The first one requires more mental effort, for sure!

A truly confident person doesn't accept victimhood. It simply doesn't exist in their reality. You choose how you feel, and nobody can make you feel bad except yourself.

So, from now on, no more complaining such as:

-"*She* made me feel bad" ;
-"*He* made me feel inadequate";
-"*They* made me feel inferior"!

It doesn't exist in your new reality of Authentic Self Confidence. It's out of your vocabulary, thoughts, and energetic field!

Empowering questions:

-What do I choose?
-Do I want other people to make me feel bad?
-Do I choose to feel bad myself?
-Why would I choose to lower my vibration?

You can choose to be a driver or a passenger. So, why not be fully in charge of your journey and destination?

Whenever I feel triggered, I say to myself: "Elena, leave it *energetically*. It's not worth it. "

And I simply choose to let it go. At the beginning of my journey, I found the EFT Tapping (Emotional Freedom Technique) to be incredibly helpful for calming down, relaxing, and releasing trapped energies. *The Tapping Solution* by Nick Ortner is an excellent book for beginners and, if applied correctly, can give you almost instant emotional freedom and release. It's also a tool you can use regularly.

My old self would often get angry or even lash out at people (because I chose to stay in a victim vibe and didn't know how to relax my nervous system and release my triggers). Now, it's just a thing of the past, and I still use EFT tapping on myself daily. It's of the best discoveries I've made. I believe that authentically confident people take responsibility for how they react to different triggers and situations, and they are a master of their emotions. From my experience- reading or learning about emotions was never as helpful as applying the EFT tapping technique on myself. I genuinely believe that if everyone used it on themselves daily, the world would be a better and more peaceful place. It all starts with you, and I hope you'll give my recommendation a try.

But it's not so much about a given modality. There are many modalities that can help us calm our nerves, heal, manage our emotions, release negative energy, or relax. For example, Reiki, the Sedona Method, and zillions of meditations you could do. Choose the modality you enjoy and stick with it.

What really matters is the mindset behind using these modalities. And our mindset should be that of a victor who takes responsibility for their life and is willing to learn, grow, practice, and improve. I believe that if a person is not ready to help themselves and is in a victim mindset, you can give them the best and fastest modality out there, and they will still find fault with it and blame their circumstances on other people. And I'll be the first to admit that I used to be a bit like that too! I was a "halfway Elena", never going entirely into what I wanted to master. I repeated the same pattern with business ventures, writing projects, other creative ventures, health and diets, fitness programs, and healing modalities. But when I discovered tapping, I promised myself I would dive fully in and stick to one book or program until it worked. And the book *The Tapping Solution* definitely worked for me, and so did similar programs about tapping.

What really changed was my mindset and energy. I was ready to transform myself from within myself. As they say: "when the student is ready, the teacher appears"! So, whether you decide to expand what you discover with this book, with EFT Tapping, or a similar healing modality, let's remind ourselves once again that an authentically confident person takes responsibility and accountability seriously. They know that mindset is everything and nobody can do their inner work for them.

They focus all their ability on creating the life they desire, starting with themselves. They choose the responsibility of letting go vs. taking things personally. So, what does it really mean to take things personally? Well...to take things personally means you literally take something and allow it to stay in your personal vibration...

Why not choose to let go? *Instead of taking things personally, you can choose to let them go...personally!*

At the same time, be open to receiving lessons and feedback. But always consider the source! If a person who offers you feedback does embody what you desire and is living proof of what is possible, chances are their feedback will be a valuable tool to help you improve whatever it is you're working on.

An authentically confident person is not defensive and uses feedback to grow and expand. Full ownership also means welcoming our limiting beliefs instead of avoiding them or resisting them. If there's any area in your life where you can't get results, no matter how hard you try, you most likely have a limiting belief or block in that area. An authentically confident person is not afraid to face what is.

"What we resist, persists"- Carl Jung

If we allow our limiting beliefs to take hold of our reality, they only get bigger. Pay attention to what you try to avoid or resist. In my case, it was...writing! Yes, I know, I know. I've said many times that writing is my biggest passion and fuel... I don't know how I could ever live without it.

But for so many years, I kept resisting it because I feared judgment. It's pretty bizarre, isn't it? But so many people fall into similar negative patterns. Instead of staying committed to doing what they love, they resist it and find a zillion excuses to do something else.

It's time to embrace curiosity and face your limiting beliefs. Once again, you can't blame anybody for them. We entered this chapter through a space of no blame or guilt. Blame and guilt no longer exist in our space now. So...

Letting go of our limiting beliefs is so much easier!

In my previous books, *Expect to Manifest* and *Manifesting Alignment*, I mentioned my recent discovery about limiting beliefs, which may seem against the grain to some, but works great for me...

We don't need to know *why* we have a limiting belief.
It's not necessary at all. Yes, it may be helpful, but, from my personal experience it's not required. As of now, I base my inner work on releasing my limiting beliefs and other negative internal states without trying to figure out where they came from. It saves me a lot of time and energy. Instead of dwelling on your past, you can focus your energy on creating lasting transformation. But once again, please note that it's merely my way of doing things, based on my personal "inner testing", and your way may be different. I also recognize that some people may benefit from knowing *what* caused their limitations and blocks.
(Hence my earlier recommendation of seeking professional therapy/counselling, that I know, may be very healing in some circumstances).

Now, back to the process of Authentic Confidence and becoming your own curious detective of limiting beliefs...

Here's the process I recommend. Write down:

-Your fears

....
....
....

-What makes you uncomfortable

....
....
....

-Your biggest desires that are still not manifest

....
....
....

Don't rush through this process. Give yourself some time. Some people might need a mindset coach or energy healer to uncover their hidden limiting beliefs. It all depends on your personal situation. Sometimes you can spot your limiting beliefs pretty quickly and all by yourself. But sometimes, you may need a coach, which may be an excellent investment because you will save yourself a lot of time on being stuck in self-sabotage (speaking from my experience here!).

In most cases, you will find a connection between your fears, things that make you uncomfortable and goals that never manifested into your reality...

Allow yourself to feel your feelings. Don't avoid them, don't suppress them, and don't try to be "fake-positive". Positivity needs to be authentic. We already concluded that fake positivity leads nowhere.

Why apply perfume on a body that needs a shower?
Weird comparison, but it does a great job of exposing fake positivity. What we want is authentic positivity that leads to profound transformations.

When you discover your biggest fears and what makes you uncomfortable, the best course is to take action. Small, consistent daily action. This is what I did with my writing.

My first goal was process-based. I focused on writing for thirty minutes every day. It seemed easy and doable to stick to, and it helped me become a consistent writer. You can apply the same mindset and strategy to whatever scares you, for example, making videos, exercising, learning a new language, improving a skill, or starting a side business. Yes, thirty minutes a day is a great place to start and get your subconscious mind to work for you, not against you. As you get used to thirty minutes a day of working on your fears, you become more confident and can keep expanding and growing.

Commitment, consistency, and challenging yourself are what I like to call **the mighty Tripple C Team**! Commitment comes from taking action in the right direction, in alignment with your goals. Working on your fears and outgrowing them by taking positive action is part of this process. Consistency helps build momentum, transform your mindset and align your energy with what you want by getting closer to it every day.

Finally, challenge stimulates authentic growth. So, challenge yourself to expand your comfort zone, little by little, every day. It doesn't have to be a high-water jump. If you're terrified of something, a high-water jump may even traumatize you and increase your fears.

The only way to overcome darkness is to shine a light on it. Regularly self-reflect on your limiting beliefs, inner blocks, fears, or things you're ashamed of. You can manifest an incredible life by releasing your limitations and letting go of what no longer serves you. The process is always the same!

Identify:

-Your fears

-What makes you uncomfortable

-Your biggest desires that are still not manifest

You can write down your goals and desires and then self-reflect on your limiting beliefs around them, in other words, identify the beliefs and fears that prevent you from taking action, be it physical, mental, or emotional. Keep auditing and releasing your shadows. Don't mask them. Use them as a compass that leads you to something better. Embrace the power of transforming negative into positive. Become an example of what is possible and share your story with others. The world needs more compassionate, loving, and authentically confident leaders who inspire people to change and transform without shaming or guilt-tripping. And it all starts with you and your inner work.

Chapter 5 The Best Way to Save Your Precious Mental, Spiritual and Emotional Energy (and use it to manifest your desires with ease!)

Let's expand on what we learned in the previous chapter about self-belief and conviction. You need to focus on what you really desire, what's in your heart. Most likely, it's accompanied by all kinds of "buts" and excuses.

You may think it will take too long. But guess what…Time will pass anyway! So, think about where you will be in five years from now, if you just start working on your goal or desire. Start moving forward right here, right now.

We're not concerned about what's realistic based on other people's beliefs and opinions. This can only get you so far!
Now, yes, of course, some circumstances may require an opinion of a professional. This is pretty common sense.
But we're talking about your life's vision here, not so much about solving problems that need expert advice.

We are creating a new life vision for you from a new paradigm. It's never too late to start planting your garden of happiness, abundance, and inner freedom.

Re-connect with your burning desire for authentic success fueled by a favorable decision to be in alignment and act with passion and confidence.

In the last chapter, we entered a reality with no guilt or judgment. Now, we're adding a new layer of a reality where there are no "buts" and no excuses. So, the only job you have to do, for now, is to give yourself some time and space to decide what you really want based on your heart's desires and nothing else.

You're not trying to be practical or realistic, although you can if that's what you desire. Everyone's different. Change your relationship with obstacles. They are opportunities in disguise, so train yourself to see them.

Have I already told you about your new "job responsibilities"? Focus on the positive and release the need to complain. There's no such thing as blaming or complaining. If you feel a negative emotion, recognize it for what it is, welcome it, and thank it because it's showing you to release something, and then let it go!

The following journaling exercise to guide you through this process:

-What is your mission?

-What do you desire to transform about yourself, your community, and the world?

-What is your vision?

-Do you have a vision of an ideal world?

-Can you live and embody it while respecting yourself, your freedom, and other people's freedom too?

-What is your why?

-What is important to you and why?

Once again, there are no "buts" and no excuses.

I recently shared this process with a friend who wanted to manifest love. She expressed her desire to attract a man into her life and was very specific. But then...yes, you guessed, she went on an "oh but" trip...

-"All good, caring men are taken...."
-"It's hard to meet someone if you're over forty...."

Most of her mental energy was focused on "buts," limiting beliefs and excuses...And we all do this! This is why, daily inner work is so important. I'm a big believer in auditing your thoughts daily through mindful self-reflection, meditation, or journaling.

I've also been guilty of an excuse mindset so many times! And it only slowed my progress and made me scared of taking action. For example, for years, I had the desire to start a blog, but I had so many buts and excuses, such as:

-"It's too late to start. ";

-"Blogging is dead in 2020." (by the way, they say this every year, haha!);

-"Nobody will read my blog; what if I get a hater? "

And so on and so forth...But then I realized that I wasn't acting on my own authority. I put other people's experiences, opinions, and beliefs before my passion.

Because when you really want to do something or have a strong desire in your heart, it means it's there for a reason. You have a bigger purpose, moving towards it will fill your life with joy! Yes, some projects might be more challenging, and some goals might take longer to achieve. But, if you do what you love, the mere process will energize you. Remember to act on making decisions on your own behalf! Be like a curious detective.

Here's the little secret: Your desire must be bigger than your "buts" and excuses.

There is a surface purpose versus a profound purpose. A surface purpose might be something like making a living from your passion. It can be a great place to start. But we can get so much deeper into our purpose because it's our purpose that keeps us going.

Create a purpose that makes you want to cry out of joy. See yourself as the influential leader that you are. For example, your desire and a surface-level purpose might be to make a living from your passion. Or perhaps to develop your skills and talents. Which is great!

But you can dive deeper and think about the lives you will *positively impact* with your work. You can visualize the people you will help and how their lives and family lives will be transformed forever. If you're into karma and spirituality, you can imagine an energetic compound effect your actions will have on this planet. I don't know about you, but visualizing happy readers is my biggest fuel and motivation!

Chapter 6 Becoming Your Own Leader, Guru, and Teacher

Your thoughts and beliefs can either limit you or help you grow. You are your filter, and you decide what you let into your mind.

When we don't feel worthy of love, happiness, and abundance, we don't know who we are. We lose authenticity and confidence. Instead, we get too attached to external validation and achievement and what others say or think of us. Sometimes, we may even project unworthy feelings onto others, sabotaging their authentic self-confidence.

Unworthiness is self-destructive, keeps us stuck in the same patterns, and prevents us from creating a meaningful life.
On the other hand, worthiness makes us achieve and stay motivated because we are led by our own values and choices. When you feel worthy, you control what's inside you and what you choose to radiate into the world. It comes from the core of your being. There's nothing to prove, nothing to defend, and nothing to explain. When you embody worthiness, you are your own leader and teacher.

Sure, you are open to learning from others. But since you know who you are, you always find great mentors or teachers, people who resonate with you and can help you grow while sharing similar values.

Investing in wrong teachers was a big pattern I kept manifesting when I didn't feel worthy. When I say: "wrong teachers", I don't mean that their teachings didn't have any value. The problem was that we were not aligned and that I always ignored my intuition. In fact, it felt like I'd lost it!

I often bragged about how much I paid for a given program. I wanted to be seen as someone who is not afraid of investing in herself. But I never got any results and was stuck in a shiny object syndrome cycle. At some point, I even developed a limiting belief that everything was a scam...

Looking back, I know my actions were dictated by the fear of missing out or not being enough. I didn't have enough awareness to dive into my true feelings and motivations.
These days, however, whenever I invest in a new program or teacher, I know I have made the right decision because I use my own authentic values as a judge. I don't invest in something that doesn't resonate with me, and I don't want to learn from a teacher with a radically different set of values.

I invest in myself from a place of wholeness or worthiness, not from a fear of missing out, chasing trends, or keeping up with the Joneses. I'm referring to mindsets such as: "What if other people in my industry took this program and they are successful, and I am stuck with no success?"

As with everything, worthiness is a journey that takes daily practice and commitment. Become aware of your inner states and how you feel when you invest in yourself.

When you decide you are worthy of all the good stuff life has to offer, you open your internal door to start receiving. You no longer doubt yourself and know you have enough energy and capacity to follow through with any program of your choice and can manifest the results you deserve.

But when you stay in the energy of trying to explain yourself and prove yourself, you block yourself from receiving.

Your embodiment of unworthiness contradicts your wants and desires. It's sad but true. It was my reality for so long. I only wish I'd known this sooner!

Worthiness also connects to your boundaries and how you communicate them to others with your *actions*. You are worthy of respect because you *respect yourself*. Why would you allow anyone to disrespect you?

Communicate your boundaries to yourself and the Universe first. Then embody them. Chances are you will not need to explain them to anyone around you. As you choose to embody what you believe in, people will react to you differently. Internal worthiness often connects to abundance and how much abundance you can receive. Stop chasing external opportunities. Instead, ask yourself: *what would I like to do?* Start moving forward as soon as you can and embrace the power of practical learning. For example, when I set up my blog, I had no idea about SEO (search engine optimization). I began to pick it up as I immersed myself in the process of blogging. As Marie Forleo puts it beautifully:

"Everything is figureoutable!"

Create your own process and way of doing things and be known for that. Stop basing your decisions on what others are doing. What they choose is based on their beliefs, mindset, and energy. Everyone is unique, so follow your way! There's only *one* step in this process- it's all about making up your mind and sticking to it every day! Small, consistent actions taken from a place of joy and good energy lead to massive results (and many positive, unexpected manifestations along the way!).

Whenever I teach and share about worthiness, I can't skip the topic of self-care & boundaries. As an empath and healer, I attract many like-minded people through my books. And I know many of my empathic readers will be fired up to get started working on their true desires and purposes, which often includes being in service to others, whether it's through healing work, coaching, or artistic endeavors. But, even if you don't fall into the above category, you will benefit hugely from reflecting on your self-care routine and boundaries. No matter what your profession or purpose is.

As I'm sure, you already know and have heard many times:

You can't help others when you're not well.

Yes, nothing new here, I know! The actual game begins when we choose to embody this mindset daily by sticking to our energetic boundaries and an effective self-care routine.

If you want to help others and shine your light, make sure your cup is full. Like really fully full!

But what exactly is self-care?

And what does it have to do with energetic boundaries...?
By choosing your self-care routine and activities and sticking to your plan, you radiate the magnetic energy of: "I am worthy of taking care of myself, and I use my time wisely."

Also, by respecting your rules and choosing yourself, other people will treat you differently. Oh, not to mention the most enormous rewards- achieving progress with your self-care routine and showing up as your best self physically, mentally, emotionally, and spiritually. When you see the results of your self-care boundaries, you feel like you are reaching the next level. Self-care can be many things, and it's all about choosing what works for you based on your goals, lifestyle, free time, and interests.

Oh, and let me stress that it's not about telling others how committed you are. It's about *doing it* yourself and setting an example. Of course, if you live with family or roommates, you may want to tell them about your new self-care routine, habits, or hobbies. But don't do it in a crusade-like style.

What's a crusade style, you may ask?

Let me give you an example from my own life. Several years ago, I discovered what, as you already know, is one of my favorite healing modalities - EFT Tapping. I experienced

terrific results with it, so naturally, I felt like telling all my family and friends about this unusual tapping discovery.
But I was too pushy and acted with "my way is the only way" convincing energy.

Luckily, I quickly realized I was doing something wrong and stopped. Instead, I focused my energy on learning more about EFT and practicing it for myself. My partner was the only person involved in my tapping routine. I told him that every evening I needed an hour to do my inner work and that I was doing this tapping thing and really enjoying it.

Very soon, he told me: "Yea, I can tell it's working for you. Your energy is so much calmer. I might give it a go as well! What can I use it for? Can I use it to be more productive?"

Then, I began getting similar feedback from family, friends, and colleagues. This time, I wasn't trying to convince anyone or make them feel like they had to do what I was doing because otherwise, their lives would be miserable.

I finally learned how to fully embody what I was doing. And after staying consistent with my routine (I still tap on myself daily, and it's my favorite self-care routine because it makes everything else so much easier for me!), I could finally help and inspire others.

So, no more "self-help crusades" or convincing. Simply schedule your favorite self-care activities and do them. Embody them and enjoy the progress!

Here are different examples of self-care activities:

-Cooking healthy meals, making juices and smoothies. If you stick to daily nutritional improvements, your biggest reward will be more energy, vitality, and health. And you will set a great example to your loved ones (without trying to convince them that your diet is the best because, at the end of the day, it's all about creating a healthy lifestyle and diet that works for you and everyone is different);

-Reading books, learning a new language, or new skills. Even half an hour a day can compound into mastering a new skill or language. You will feel mentally active and energized! Plus, it feels so good to experience progress!

-Meditation, prayer, studying spirituality – these activities are great to help you cultivate inner peace and connect to something bigger;

-Going to a spa, getting a massage, or treating yourself to a nice bath – all these activities are incredibly relaxing and can help you disconnect, recharge, and refuel;

-Signing up for classes or taking up a new hobby – this could be learning how to play an instrument, sing, paint or make furniture, whatever you enjoy!;

-Going for a walk and listening to podcasts and audiobooks. This is one of my favorite self-care practices that I do at least three times a week. I get the benefit of moving my body and burning calories while learning new things, opening my mind, and enjoying nature.

Don't make a lack of time an excuse. Start off with a new belief that you are worthy of self-care, because you *are*!

Respect yourself and your boundaries by creating a self-care plan in your mind first. Then, write it down. Create a self-care system or routine based on your interests, goals, and lifestyle. Then, embody your new decisions, enjoy your progress and inspire others just by being you and doing what you love. Allow self-care to make you shine because you're worth it!

Chapter 7 When Negative Voices in Your Head Can No Longer Control You (and the simple mindset shift to be unstoppable!)

"Who am I to be doing this…?"

"What if they don't like it…?" We all get these negative voices in our heads sometimes. And while I don't think it's possible to get rid of them completely, once and for all (even the most successful people have these voices), it's possible to re-direct them to something more positive and empowering.

Authentically confident people are aware enough to catch and transform all the negativity going on inside them into positive self-talk that is much more meaningful. I mean, since you talk to yourself anyway…Why not use your time and energy on more self-empowering questions?

As Tony Robbins puts it beautifully: "Quality questions create a quality life. Successful people ask better questions, and as a result, they get better answers."

Negative thoughts indicate that it's time to take charge of your inner dialogue and keep going! You are an authentic leader, so you can lead your inner voice in alignment with your desire. And you're definitely NOT your negative self-talk and self-imposed limitations and fears. You are an infinite being having a temporary experience here on Earth.

You came here to have a good time, learn, share, motivate and inspire. Having this approach, we simply can't succumb to negative voices in our heads. These voices are just feedback for us to reclaim our power! Negative thoughts and voices in our heads have no more control over us.

It's funny how I used to think I could either have a bad or good day. And that if I had a bad day, I couldn't do anything about it. It used to be normal to me. My family and friends would also tell me how they were "having a bad day".

But now, since I am on the journey of authenticity, I am so much more aware of what's going on inside me. Of course, I am still on a journey, I will never claim I am a guru expert, but I know today I am better than yesterday.

So, here's the most empowering part, which dawned on me recently while on a hike. I no longer have "bad days". Not even bad hours. I can have "a bad minute". Bad fifteen minutes is as far as it can go. And I've trained myself to shift out of these funky states as fast as possible. When you're authentically confident, you are your own guru and motivator. You are your cheerleader, so even if you get lost or fall down, you know how to brush yourself off and get up quickly!

A negative thought in my head is simply a reminder to look deeper from a place of curiosity and quickly nip it in the bud with love and self-compassion. When you start releasing all the inauthentic layers imposed on you by other people's standards, or your own need for approval, becoming in charge of your thoughts will be much easier!

You will realize that there was nothing to fear to begin with. The only thing you can fear is fear itself. Why would you make such a choice?

Here's another thing you can start to practice. It may be hard to do at first. I got this as a little suggestion from an old colleague, and I began to incorporate it into my life while slowly working through self-imposed fears and limitations.

So, what was it, you may ask? It's simple! The first step was to be 100% honest with myself and acknowledge *exactly* what I felt and why. This may seem easy for people who have been on the path of self-development for a while, but back then, it was all new to me, and I was so stuck in self-imposed inauthentic layers that I no longer knew who I was and what I really felt. I would pretend to be someone else, even when I was alone with myself. Then, I slowly began telling other people how I felt and why. Yet a part of me would still try to protect myself. I felt like hiding all the time!

So, slowly but surely, I began expressing my true feelings to those close to me. For example, a family member would always judge me and tell me that I had worked too much. And so, whenever I could not make it to see her, for whatever reason, I had this fear: "What if she starts judging me again and calls me a workaholic?"

This may seem ridiculous, but I still had a strong fear of being judged back then. Once I overcame that fear by owning who I was and what I wanted to do, something magical happened.

On one occasion, when I could not make it to a family gathering, I told her: "Look, I am sorry I can't make it. But driving to your place would take too much time now. I have an important project to finish. I've wanted to do it for a very long time. So, I'll be working this weekend. I know you will understand, and I hope to see you soon!"

First of all, I was honest and didn't make any excuses, such as that I wasn't feeling well or whatnot. I shared the real reason I couldn't make it and that my projects were important to me. I also didn't spend any time justifying myself or protecting myself from an imaginary "attack".

Why would someone attack me? I mean, "to attack" is a serious word, and to me it means someone literally attacks me. So, by understanding this part, I allowed myself to be safe! It's not that someone would break in and attack me because I allowed myself to be me and expressed my real reasons for not doing something?

So, by giving my family an honest reply, without hiding anything or trying to explain myself too much, something magical happened. They stopped judging me! They were kind and understanding. They replied: "Oh, congratulations, so happy you're enjoying your work. You're welcome to visit us anytime! Or let us know if you prefer to meet somewhere else, whenever you're not busy."

Now, don't get me wrong. This shift in my behavior required lots of inner work, awareness and practice. But the results were worth it! I could finally be myself and gain other people's respect without even trying. At the end of the day, my main focus was on authentic honesty. I wasn't trying to gain external validation.

After analyzing all the beautiful changes in my life, I realized that one fundamental mindset shift I made was that I gave other people permission to be themselves. Because when you are yourself, you are OK with people being themselves.

So, I no longer fear: "What if I say this, and they think that" or: "They will tell me this or that, or they will judge me." Instead, I focus on myself and redefine my values. What I am is what others can see and feel. This is the journey of authenticity.

I've been testing these concepts for several years now. And from my experience, whenever I choose to live by my rules and values and own who I am, the negative thoughts of worry and fear, such as what others will think of me, vanish away!

When you live in constant fear, you project your fears onto others, and no wonder they judge you or reflect or even confirm your own insecurities. So, try it yourself. First, give yourself some time to express your true feelings and motivations to yourself. Daily journaling is great for that. Then, when you're ready, start doing the same with other people. Don't explain too much, and don't provide any lengthy justifications. If you speak in such a way that you expect judgment or criticism, you will most likely attract it. Instead, communicate with inner confidence without seeking any permission or approval. Remember that it's safe to be you!

Depending on your current situation, this may seem like a challenging task to do, and I can totally understand. That's where I am coming from. But trust me, my friend, when you stick to the lessons from this book and go through them several times, something in your consciousness will begin to shift.

My teachings are both practical and metaphysical. They are practical because they give you something to do and practice as you read my books. So, you can get started immediately, no matter where you're coming from. And with enough repetition, your consciousness will elevate to a new level. And so, you will discover a beautiful, metaphysical element that feels truly magical. The practical part is to be done, internalized, and embodied. The metaphysical part will create itself as you keep elevating your consciousness.

So, never stop doing this work. Those who keep going activate the compound effect of inner work and are amazed at how wonderful their lives get.

I can't wait to hear about your transformation and success story!

Until next time we "meet,"

Sending you lots of love,

Elena

Your friend and guide in conscious manifesting

Join Our Manifestation Newsletter and Get a Free eBook

To help you amplify what you've learned in this book, I'd like to offer you a free copy of my LOA Workbook – a powerful, 5-day program (eBook & audio) designed to help you raise your vibration while eliminating resistance and negativity.

To sign up for free, visit the link below now:

www.loaforsuccess.com/newsletter

You'll also get free access to my inspirational LOA Newsletter to help you stay high vibe!

Through this email newsletter, I regularly share all you need to know about the manifestation mindset and energy.

Plus, whenever I release a new book, you can get it at a deeply discounted price.

To sign up for free, visit the link below or scan the code.

www.loaforsuccess.com/newsletter

If you happen to have any technical issues with your sign-up, please email us at:

support@LOAforSuccess.com

More by Elena G. Rivers:

369 Manifesting Guided Journal

Now available on Amazon:

Manifesting Alignment: Secrets to Becoming a Vibrational Match to Your Desires

Manifestation Meditation: It's Time to Meditate to Attract Your Best Life (Because You Can!)

www.ingramcontent.com/pod-product-compliance
Lightning Source LLC
Chambersburg PA
CBHW072102110526
44590CB00018B/3274